Nutrition

The Food
Pyramid

Kristin Petrie

ABDO
Publishing Company

visit us at
www.abdopub.com

Published by ABDO Publishing Company, 4940 Viking Drive, Edina, Minnesota 55435.
Copyright © 2004 by Abdo Consulting Group, Inc. International copyrights reserved in all
countries. No part of this book may be reproduced in any form without written permission from
the publisher.

Printed in the United States.

Cover Photo: Corbis
Interior Photos: Corbis pp. 1, 4, 7, 8-9, 12, 13, 17, 19, 21, 23, 24, 25, 27, 29; Corel Photo Disc p.
    16; Painet pp. 11, 15; The American Institute for Cancer Research p. 28; U.S. Department of
    Agriculture and U.S. Department of Health and Human Services pp. 5, 14, 18, 20, 24

Editors: Kate A. Conley, Stephanie Hedlund, Kristianne E. Vieregger
Art Direction: Neil Klinepier

Library of Congress Cataloging-in-Publication Data

Petrie, Kristin, 1970-
    The food pyramid / Kristin Petrie.
        p. cm. -- (Nutrition)
    Includes index.
    Summary: Discusses the five food groups that are essential to a healthy diet and how to
determine how much of each to eat.
    ISBN 1-59197-403-8
        1. Nutrition--Juvenile literature. 2. Food habits--Juvenile literature. [1. Nutrition. 2.
Food.] I. Title. II. Nutrition (Edina, Minn.)

QP141.P455 2003
613.2--dc21

2002043622

Contents

The Food Guide Pyramid

Nutrition is a complicated business. You've read about carbohydrates, protein, fat, vitamins, and minerals. You've heard a lot of conflicting information from people around you and on television. You may feel overwhelmed. How can you possibly remember so much?

You don't have to. The Food Guide Pyramid can be used as a guide for daily eating. It was developed by the United States Department of Agriculture to help you put all this information in its place, and on your plate.

Making healthy food choices is important at any age!

The pyramid shows you the foods to aim for when making food choices. When you do this, you'll be giving your body the materials it needs to keep growing. It will also heal your bumps and bruises, help you do well in school, and give you energy for work and play.

The Food Guide Pyramid

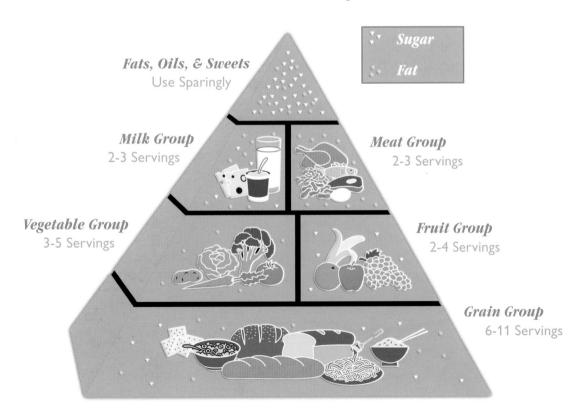

Why a Pyramid?

In the past, four food groups were used to make food choices. This was a good way to prevent nutrient **deficiencies**. The Food Guide Pyramid, however, goes a bit further. It shows a way of eating that helps you get all your nutrients. This makes your body strong and can even help prevent **cancer**, **osteoporosis**, and heart disease.

In the Food Guide Pyramid, the five food groups and the fats, oils, and sweets category are stacked on top of one another in four levels. This shows the best way to choose foods when you eat. Most foods should be from the grain, fruit, and vegetable groups. These groups pack in the most nutrients per bite.

Next, add the milk and meat food groups. They provide calcium and protein for your growing body. Lastly, enjoy the fats, oils, and sweets category. Its foods are okay in moderation, after you've given your body the nutrients it needs.

What Are Nutrients?

Nutrients are substances found in food. Your body uses nutrients in many ways. They help your body grow. They also help your body maintain and repair itself.

Fast food is usually fried in fat, which is at the top of the pyramid, so it should not be eaten often.

What would this pyramid be like if we turned the food order around? For example, what if we put the fats, oils, and sweets category closer to the base, and the grain, fruit, and vegetable groups on top? It would topple over! The pyramid wouldn't be strong or balanced, and neither would your body.

It's up to you to give your body the best foods you can find. Unfortunately, many people don't realize how an unbalanced diet affects them. Americans often eat too few nutrient-dense foods, and too many foods from the pyramid's top. This makes a very wobbly pyramid and a poor foundation for health.

Empty Calories

Have you ever heard someone say a candy bar has empty calories? That's because it has many calories but few nutrients. Many of the foods from the fats, oils, and sweets category have empty calories. That's why they should be eaten sparingly.

The food choices you make affect the way your body works. French fries affect your body in unhealthy ways because of their empty calories.

Serving Sizes

When making food choices, it is important to understand serving sizes. For example, the Food Guide Pyramid says you should eat 6 to 11 servings from the grain group each day. That sounds like a lot of breads and cereals. However, once you know what a pyramid serving size is, you will see that these servings add up quickly.

Pyramid servings are usually much smaller than typical American servings of just about anything! For example, just one ounce of breakfast cereal is one serving from the grain group. The amount you eat varies depending on the kind of cereal. Cereal such as Rice Krispies weighs very little, so one ounce may be a full cup. On the other hand, cereal such as Grape Nuts is very dense. Therefore, one ounce may be just half a cup!

Test It Out!

The next time you have breakfast cereal, pour your usual amount into a bowl. Then find a kitchen scale. Weigh your cereal before adding the milk. Remember to subtract the weight of the bowl. You may be surprised at how many grain servings you have filled just at breakfast.

Servings of rice and pasta also add up quickly. Just half a cup of these cooked foods equals one pyramid serving. A typical helping is probably closer to two to three cups, equaling six servings of carbohydrates in the grain group!

To make things more confusing, pyramid serving sizes differ from the ones you see on most food labels. Those serving sizes are closer to the amounts that people actually eat. Why the seemingly small pyramid servings? Because when you take smaller servings, there is room in your daily intake for variety. More variety in your diet gives you more types of nutrients.

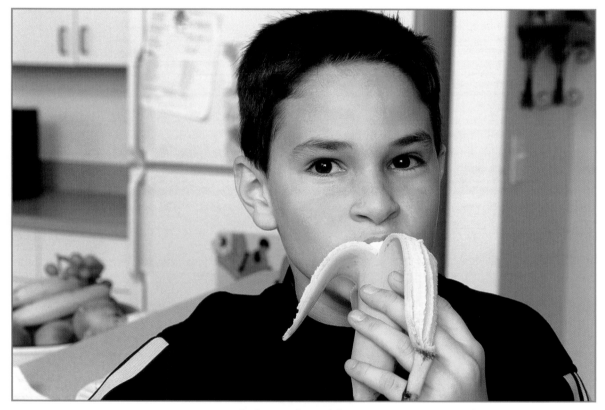

Bananas are a good choice for adding variety to your diet.

Choosing Variety

How can you add variety to your diet? Here's an example. Instead of eating a large bagel, you could choose to eat half of it. This allows you to enjoy the bagel, and you still have room for a piece of fruit and a glass of milk. This variety adds more nutrients for the same amount of calories.

Grains

Samples of a Pyramid Serving from the Grain Group

- 1 slice of bread
- 1 medium potato
- 1 small bagel or English muffin
- 1 small tortilla
- 1 ounce of ready-to-eat cereal
- ½ cup of cooked cereal, rice, pasta, or grain

What Are Carbohydrates?

Carbohydrates are nutrients. They are the body's main source of energy. Most foods contain carbohydrates in small amounts.

The base of the Food Guide Pyramid is the grain group. This group is also called the carbohydrate group, since these foods are rich in carbohydrates.

When you choose breads, pastas, and other foods from this group, aim for **whole grain** products. Whole grain products include whole wheat breads, bagels, and pastas. Brown rice and

Cereal, rice, and bread are some
examples of the grain group.

fortified cereals are also **whole grain** products. These foods contain many more vitamins, minerals, and fiber than white bread, white rice, and sugary cereals contain.

Nutrients from the grain group also include the B vitamins. They are used to make energy for playing, running, and thinking. They also help you fight off germs and infections. And, B vitamins keep your **nerves** tuned so you can blink, smile, and kick!

Recently, carbohydrates have had a bad reputation. So, hearing that this food group should be the base of your diet may be confusing. The truth about carbohydrates is the same about any food! Eating too many carbohydrates that contain empty **calories** is unhealthy. In fact, too many poor choices from any food group can lead to **obesity**, **diabetes**, and heart disease.

Pasta is a grain product.

Help with the shopping by choosing healthy foods, such as whole grain breads.

Vegetables & Fruits

Samples of a Pyramid Serving from the Vegetable & Fruit Groups

Vegetable Group:
- 1 cup (about four leaves) of lettuce, spinach, broccoli, or other leafy greens
- ½ cup of cooked or raw vegetables
- ¾ cup of vegetable juice

Fruit Group:
- 1 medium apple, orange, or similar fruit
- 1 medium banana
- ½ cup of chopped, cooked, or canned fruit
- ¾ cup of fruit juice

Vegetables and fruits join the grain group to form the base of a healthy diet. They are great sources of carbohydrates. And, research shows that people who have grains, fruits, and vegetables as the base of their diet are the healthiest. Why?

These foods are packed with nutrients that keep your body strong, from your bones and muscles all the way down to your cells. They also protect you from illnesses and diseases. And, when you eat more of these foods, you have less room on your plate for foods with empty **calories**.

Fruits are full of vitamins and minerals. They are a good choice for snack time!

Three to five servings of vegetables are recommended. That's because vegetables contain many vitamins, minerals, and other nutrients. One of the nutrients in many vegetables is vitamin A, or beta-carotene. It helps you see in the dark and protects your cells from damage.

Fruits also contain nutrients, such as vitamins A and C, fiber, and **antioxidants**. Two to four servings of fruit will provide your body with what it needs. They will keep your skin moist, keep germs out, and keep your blood pressure low.

Milk & Meat

Samples of a Pyramid Serving from the Milk & Meat Groups

Milk Group:
- 1 cup of milk or yogurt
- 1½ ounces of hard cheese
- 2 ounces of processed cheese (1 to 2 slices)

Meat Group:
- 2 to 3 ounces of meat, poultry, or fish
- ½ cup of cooked, canned, or dried peas or beans
- 1 egg
- 2 tablespoons of peanut butter

What Is Protein?

Protein is a nutrient. The body uses protein to build, maintain, and repair tissues. So, protein is an important part of a healthy diet.

Meat, beans, eggs, nuts, and dairy products share the third level of the pyramid. They are in the third level together because they provide protein. They also give us similar vitamins and minerals.

These foods from the milk and meat groups are good sources of protein and fiber.

Many of the foods in these groups are dense in nutrients and **calories**. That means every bite has many nutrients and calories. So, we need fewer bites of these foods than of grains, fruits, and vegetables.

A piece of chicken or a hamburger are each equal to two to three meat servings. That means you are eating your entire meat requirement at one time! The two to three servings of meat—combined with vegetables, dairy products, and grains—will provide all the nutrients needed to build and repair your body. Healthy choices from this food group include lean meats and protein-rich foods from plants, such as dried beans and peas.

The milk group includes more than just milk! It also contains other dairy products, such as yogurt and cheese. Foods in the milk group are packed with calcium, protein, and the B vitamin **riboflavin**. Just a cup of milk and one or two slices of cheese each day will help you meet your calcium needs. Good food choices from the milk group are low-fat dairy products such as skim or one percent milk.

Milk & Meat Matters

The milk and meat groups are high on the Food Guide Pyramid. However, they are still important parts of your diet! Remember, though, that animal products contain saturated fats and cholesterol. Too much of either is unhealthy for your heart.

Opposite page: Milk contains calcium, which is very important for healthy bones and teeth. It also helps transmit nerve impulses, so you can move your arms and eyes!

Fats, Oils, & Sweets

Samples of a Pyramid Serving from the Fats, Oils, & Sweets Category

- 1 teaspoon of butter
- ½ cup of ice cream
- 1 teaspoon of sugar
- 1 tablespoon of cream cheese
- 1 teaspoon of jelly
- 12 ounces of soda or fruit drink

Foods in the fats, oils, and sweets category include butter, candy, cookies, chips, and soft drinks. Many of these add flavor and texture to foods, as well as a little fun. On the other hand, they are also a source of quick, empty **calories**, so it is important to be

Cakes, cookies, and donuts are all part of the fats, oils, and sweets category.

aware of them. While no foods are bad, too many choices from the top of the pyramid may lead to health problems.

For example, one can of soda pop has about 10 teaspoons of sugar to make it taste sweet. That's 140 **calories** toward your day's total calories, without a single vitamin or mineral! If you are an active person, you have room in your diet for some empty calories like this. But, it's best to give your body nutrients first.

Fat in sweets provides energy and helps some vitamins travel in your body. Even so, too much can cause problems.

Combination Foods

Obviously, not all foods that we eat fit neatly into one food group. Pizza, cheeseburgers, soups, and tacos are called combination foods. That's because they get their ingredients from more than one of the food groups.

Think about a taco, for example. Take it apart, and you'll find most of the food groups! The corn or flour shell is one serving from the grain group. Lettuce and tomato equal two servings from the vegetable group. Meat or beans are a serving from the meat group. And, cheese is a serving from the milk group. So, one taco means a serving from most of the pyramid's levels!

Other Combinations

Can you think of other combination foods? A ham and cheese sandwich is one. How about spaghetti and meatballs? Now, what is your favorite combination food?

Opposite page: Let's see where the food groups are in these tacos.

Vegetable Group – 4 servings

Milk Group – 2 servings

Meat Group – 2 servings

Grain Group – 2 servings

Daily Eating

Do you have to eat all of these foods every day? No, although it certainly wouldn't hurt! Everyone eats differently every day. The Food Guide Pyramid shows the amount and type of foods you should eat over a number of days. Your goal should be to eat a variety of foods from each food group to get all the nutrients your body needs.

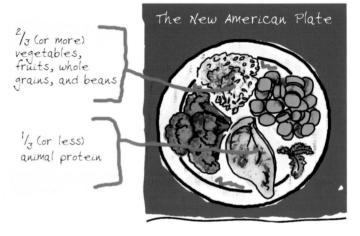

The New American Plate

$2/_3$ (or more) vegetables, fruits, whole grains, and beans

$1/_3$ (or less) animal protein

Another diagram that can help with healthy eating is called the New American Plate. It shows that grains, fruits, and vegetables make up the greatest portion of this meal. Protein-rich food, such as chicken, takes up the remaining space. Add a glass of milk and some fruit. Now you've done a great job of getting all the food groups.

You are probably already getting a balanced diet. By eating a variety of foods from the food groups every day, you are getting the nutrients your body needs.

    All of this may seem difficult. But, now that you know about serving sizes and combination foods, you're probably doing it already! Most children just need to make small changes.

    Snack time is a great time to shape up your daily intake. Instead of chips and pop, make some of your snacks more nutritious. Grab juice or milk to drink, eat a piece of fruit or a handful of baby carrots, or have some yogurt to be healthier. With a little effort, you can make sure your pyramid is balanced!

Glossary

antioxidant - a substance that protects your cells from damage.

calorie - the unit of measure for food energy.

cancer - any of a group of often deadly diseases characterized by an abnormal growth of cells that destroys healthy tissues and organs.

deficiency - a shortage of substances needed to be healthy.

diabetes - a disease in which a person's body cannot properly absorb normal amounts of sugar and starch.

fortified - having one or more nutrients not normally found in a food added to increase that food's nutritional value.

nerves - clusters of cells that the body uses to send messages to and from the brain.

nutrition - the study of nutrients and the processes of eating, digesting, absorbing, transporting, using, storing, and excreting these substances.

obesity - a condition of having too much body fat.

osteoporosis - a disease where the bones lose calcium, causing them to become weak.

riboflavin - a B vitamin found in dairy products. Riboflavin helps produce energy and promote growth.

whole grains - products that are made from grains that remain in their whole form. They have not been processed or milled and, therefore, retain their naturally occurring nutrients.

Saying It

antioxidant - an-tee-AHK-suh-duhnt
beta-carotene - BAY-tuh-KAR-uh-teen
calcium - KAL-see-uhm
carbohydrate - kahr-boh-HI-drayt
cholesterol - kuh-LES-tuh-rohl
diabetes - di-uh-BEE-teez

fortified - FOR-tuh-fyd
nutrient - NOO-tree-uhnt
obesity - oh-BEE-suh-tee
osteoporosis - ahs-tee-oh-puh-ROH-suhs
riboflavin - ri-buh-FLAY-vuhn

Web Sites

To learn more about the Food Guide Pyramid, visit ABDO Publishing Company on the World Wide Web at **www.abdopub.com**. Web sites about the pyramid and serving sizes are featured on our Book Links page. These links are routinely monitored and updated to provide the most current information available.

Index